FACT FILE

Plants

Marine plants use sunlight to help them grow, just like the plants that live on land. One kind of marine plant is seaweed. When lots of seaweed grows close together, it makes a kelp forest. **Seagrasses cover the ocean floor in some areas.**

There are also mangrove trees that grow in shallow areas with little water. **Fish and other sea creatures often eat marine plants. They can also live among them, or hide from predators among their leaves or roots.**

The Great Barrier Reef

There's lots to see at this famous Australian reef.

Great Barrier Reef Marine Park

Queensland

The Great Barrier Reef is made up of coral. It was created millions of years ago in the Coral Sea, and most of it is off the Queensland coast. It is more than 2600 km long, and can be seen from space. It is a World Heritage Site.

As well as many types of coral, the reef is home to lots of fish and marine life. Almost every sea creature in this book can be found on the reef.

Visitors like to snorkel, dive or ride in glass-bottom boats to look at the bright colours of the plants and animals.

13

Australian giant conch

Shells

Some sea creatures make and wear shells to keep them safe. Have you seen any of these?

1. AUSTRALIAN GIANT CONCH

This shell is home to the world's biggest snail – they can grow up to 60 cm long. They live in sandy, shallow water at the beach.

2. TIGER COWRY

The snail that lives in this shell crawls around rock pools all day and night. It looks pretty, but you have to be careful – this shell has very sharp edges!

3. SCORPION CONCH

A snail that eats plants lives in this shell. It has seven spines and a little peephole at the bottom of the shell to see through.

4. QUEEN FAN SCALLOP

Scallops are well known for being good tucker. Special fishermen dive down into the water to get them.

On the menu

These four food chains show who eats who in the sea.

1
Reef sharks eat parrotfish. Parrotfish eat coral.

2 Moray eels eat octopuses. Octopuses eat crabs. Crabs eat brine shrimp.

CORAL: KEVIN DEACON; BRINE SHRIMP: KEN EASTWOOD; ALL OTHERS: GETTY IMAGES

3 Tiger sharks eat loggerhead turtles. Loggerhead turtles eat squid. Squid eat shrimp.

4

Orcas eat Australian fur seals. Australian fur seals eat cuttlefish. Cuttlefish eat crabs.

Look out... sharks!

These sea creatures have been on Earth for millions of years.

Sharks have been swimming in our seas since before dinosaurs even existed. One kind of shark that lived up to 25 million years ago had teeth that were as big as your head!

Different types of shark eat different foods. Most of them are meat-eaters. They can eat fish, mammals (such as seals or dolphins), shellfish, or even other sharks. Sharks don't like the taste of humans, so they don't really hunt us.

Some sharks see very well, even in murky water, and they have an excellent sense of smell so they can easily hunt prey.

Sharks have very powerful jaws and many rows of sharp, pointy teeth.

Life on the coast

In the past, people living by the ocean found most of their food in the sea.

This tree is missing some bark. The bark may have been used to make a canoe.

Aboriginal people lived in Australia for tens of thousands of years before Europeans settled here. Many of the Aboriginal people who lived near the coast made canoes from trees. This meant they could travel by water and hunt for food in bays, rivers and the ocean.

Traditionally, indigenous people living on the coast ate seafood, including fish, turtles and shellfish. They would place discarded shells in big pile. These piles are called middens, and many still exist today. Middens are usually found near the sea.

This is a midden. Can you see the shells on the ground?

These are old stone knives and spear tips made from rocks.

In a midden you might find shellfish and campfire remains, and the bones of fish, birds, and sea mammals. There may also be tools made from stone, shells and bone.

OPP PAGE: BILL BACHMAN; THIS PAGE BOTTOM: MURRAY SPENCE, OTHER IMAGES GETTY IMAGES

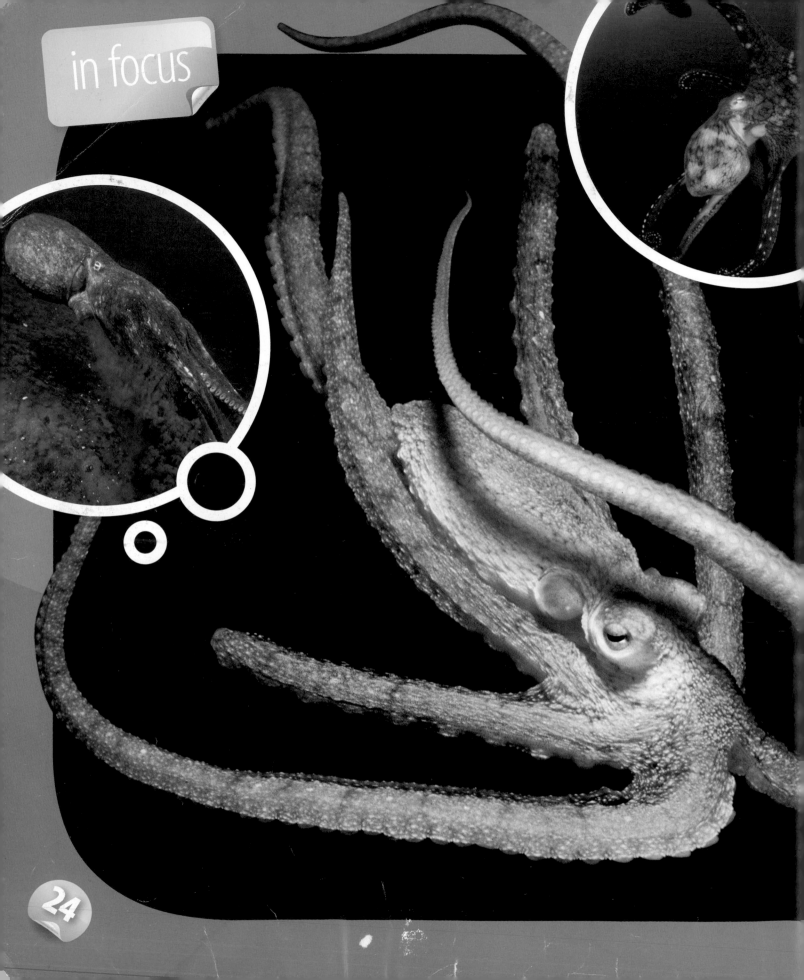

Meet an octopus

Learn all about this strange and beautiful sea creature.

Their favourite foods are crabs and molluscs.

Their predators are eels, dolphins, sharks and humans.

They have suckers on the underside of their tentacles to help them hang onto things.

Every octopus has eight tentacles. If one of these becomes damaged, the octopus can grow it back!

Female octopuses lay eggs that hatch after four to six weeks.

Octopuses usually live alone on the sea floor.

Octopuses can taste what they touch using their suction cups.

Octopuses can squirt black ink to confuse animals that are trying to catch them.

Octopuses can change their colour and shape.

They move by crawling along the ocean floor, or by swimming.

Some of the octopuses in Australia's oceans are only 10 cm long. Some have tentacles that reach up to 1 m in length.

They don't hear very well, but have very good eyesight.

Meet a
seahorse

These funny little animals are actually fish!

Seahorses can change colour to blend in with whatever is around them. This can help save them from other animals that want to eat them. They live among seaweed in shallow, warm water. Some seahorses are less than 1 cm long. Others can be up to 30 cm long!

meet a
starfish

Have you ever seen a star in the sea?

Starfish are animals that live on the rocky sea floor.
They have hundreds of tiny feet and crawl very slowly.
Starfish eat oysters, coral, fish and other animals.
They turn their stomachs inside out to eat.
There are more than 2000 species of
starfish in the world.

Danger in the water

Some of them may look friendly, but you don't want to touch these creatures!

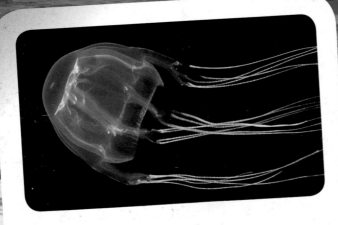

BOX JELLYFISH

All jellyfish sting their prey with venom, but not all jellyfish can harm humans. The most dangerous to humans is the box jellyfish. It has long tentacles that can reach up to 3 m long, and a powerful venom that can kill humans.

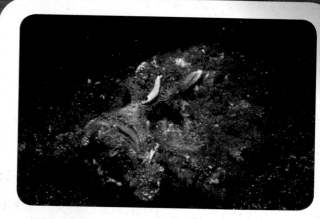

STONEFISH

This fish has 13 sharp, venomous spines on its back. It rests on the sea floor to easily catch shrimp and fish to eat. It blends into its environment so well, that humans risk stepping on it and being stung.

Remember: never touch an animal in the wild!

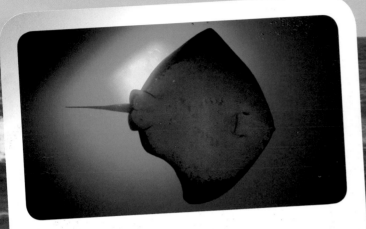

STINGRAYS

The stingray is the largest venomous fish in the world. It usually swims away from predators if it's scared, but can also use its pointed, venomous tail to defend itself. Stingrays like to sit on the sandy ocean floor, but this means humans can accidentally step on them, which may cause the ray to sting them.

BLUE-RINGED OCTOPUS

If a blue-ringed octopus feels threatened, it can defend itself by stinging other creatures with a very strong venom. When a blue-ringed octopus feels threatened, its blue rings get brighter, so you know to stay away!

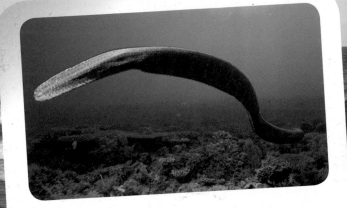

OLIVE SEA SNAKE

This snake lives in the ocean, but comes up to the surface to breathe about once every half an hour. It has poisonous venom that it can inject into its victims with its sharp fangs. It normally doesn't attack humans but if it's frightened it may strike.

LIONFISH

The lionfish is very pretty, but don't let that fool you! Its spikes are venomous, and if it stings you, it will hurt a lot. Luckily, their venom isn't deadly to humans. If you leave the lionfish alone, it will usually stay away from you.

CONE SNAILS

Cone snails often have very beautiful shells, but you should never pick them up. They have tiny harpoons inside their shells, and when they feel threatened, they shoot these at their attacker. The harpoons sting a lot and can be poisonous to humans.

CROCODILE

Saltwater crocodiles can swim quite far out into the ocean. They don't usually attack humans in the ocean, but if you see one, stay away from it. Some beaches in Australia have signs telling you not to swim in the sea because of the crocodiles that live there. If you see one of those signs, make sure you obey it.

Glossary

Colony A big group of coral polyps.

Coral polyp A tiny marine animal that settles in one spot with lots of other polyps, and then forms coral.

Crustaceans Hard-shelled organisms that shed their shell as they grow bigger to make way for a new shell.

Gills The part of a fish that lets them breathe.

Midden A pile of shells, bones and campfire remains, that was left near the sea by indigenous people who lived on the coast.

Murky Cloudy, foggy and difficult to see through.

Plankton Very tiny plants and animals that float in the water and make up a shrimp's diet.

Scavenger A type of animal that eats whatever food it can find.

Further reading & internet sites

Fact file: sea critters
Tony Ayling, 2006, Steve Parish Publishing.

Amazing facts about Australian marine life
Steve Parish, 1997, Steve Parish Publishing.

Under the Sea
Becca Saunders, 2008, Young Reed.

Amazing Australian reptiles, fish and amphibians
Barry Silkstone, 2004, Heinemann Library.

Ocean creatures jigsaw book
Lee Krutop, 2003, Five Miles Press.

Learn the difference between mammals, birds, fish and reptiles:

www.sheppardsoftware.com/
content/animals/quizzes/
kidscorner/animal_games_
water_surface_btn_large.html

Index